The Colour of British Rail Vol.1

DIESEL PIONEERS

ROBERT STEPHENS

The British Rail Diesel Loco Fleet up to 1970

Designed by Nigel Trevena
Printed by Century Litho, Penryn, Cornwall
Bound by Booth Bookbinders, Penryn, Cornwall

ISBN 0 906899 29 X

First published 1988

Published by
ATLANTIC TRANSPORT PUBLISHERS
Waterside House Falmouth Road
Penryn Cornwall TR10 8BE
England

Atlantic

DIESEL PIONEERS

Introduction

Following the development of its 350/400hp diesel shunters, the LMS was the first British railway company to introduce main line diesel electric locomotives, in the form of 10000/10001, 10000 leaving Derby Works in December 1947. In addition to these, H.G. Ivatt ordered the North British Locomotive 827hp locomotive 10800 in 1945. This machine was intended for medium mixed traffic and branch line work, its design closely resembling the contemporary USA design for 'switchers'. It was delivered in 1950.

The other major pioneer in the field of diesel electric traction, the Southern Railway, introduced the first of its prototypes, 10201, after nationalisation, in December 1950. The only other independent company to consider the use of main line diesels was the LNER, its scheme to introduce 25 1,600hp locomotives being abandoned upon nationalisation.

The performance of these early machines was affected drastically by the conditions under which they were forced to operate; in everyday operating terms on a steam railway system they were something of a nuisance, their failure often causing major disruptions to traffic.

In 1955, BR announced its Modernisation Plan with projected costs of £1,240 million to be spread over 15 years, a figure which in the event was greatly exceeded. A key aspect of this plan was the intention to abandon steam traction, the announcement, however, coinciding with the continuing production of 9F 2-10-0s.

Instead of introducing well proven standard designs of American construction, BR considered it to be politically preferable to place the Pilot Scheme orders with British manufacturers. This decision is now widely regarded as a serious misjudgement, incurring unnecessarily heavy costs for the British taxpayer. The 1955 plan provided for the introduction of 2,500 locomotives with initial orders for 171 machines. In 1956, for the first time, more diesel locomotives were built than steam. Several of the Pilot Scheme orders were for batches of 10 or 20 locomotives, forsaking the construction of a prototype, a mistake which BR later came to regret.

Maintenance of these early engines presented a major problem, most locomotives having to share outdated and unsuitable facilities with steam. This problem was addressed by the construction of purpose built diesel maintenance depots, the first of these being in north London at Devons Road. Most coaching stock was then not equipped for electrical train heating, so many diesel locomotives were fitted with train heating boilers, which often took their weight over the specified axle loading and restricted their route availability. Other weight problems with the early designs became apparent when working loose coupled freight, runaways occuring because of inadequate braking power, this problem being remedied by the building of specially constructed brake tenders which remained in use pending the disappearance of loose coupled freight working.

Prior to the introduction of a standard traction plan for the whole of BR, the Western Region pursued its own policy of introducing diesel hydraulic locomotives, copying the best of available German technology. However, once the standardisation policies were conceived in the mid 1960s, the hydraulics were among the first casualties of the diesel era.

With hindsight, BR would have benefitted from the evolution of standard types from its pilot scheme designs. As it was, its policies resulted in a wide variety of non-standard types of varying quality, and much time, effort and money was *wasted. However, to the enthusiast, the transition from steam was fascinating, with a number of diesel classes appearing and disappearing within a short span of years. Experiments with liveries, too, provided colourful contrasts with the grime and matt black of the ageing steam fleet, and in this book I have, where possible, portrayed the earliest liveries of each type.*

Most railway photographers reserved their film for steam survivors, and colour photographs of early diesels are scarce. I am indebted to all those who contributed irreplaceable transparencies for inclusion in this book. We all owe them our sincere thanks for recording a period fast becoming as remote as the steam age itself. Robert Stephens

FRONT COVER: After transfer from the LM to the ER, *Deltic* is emerging from Peascliffe tunnel with a Leeds to Kings Cross express in May 1959. *Photo: K.R. Pirt/K.R. Photographics*

REAR COVER, TOP: Outshopped from Crewe Works in January 1963, Western hydraulic D1044 *Western Duchess* is passing Ashchurch station on 14th September 1963. *Photo: W. Potter*

REAR COVER, BOTTOM: Newly constructed Brush/Sulzer Type 4 D1746 at Derby shed in July 1964. *Photo: T.B. Owen*

TITLE PAGE: Fresh from the paintshops, the first Peak, D1 *Scafell Pike* reposes outside the test house at Derby Works on 25th March 1959. *Photo: R.C. Riley*

LEFT: BR/Sulzer Type 2 D5251 assists Stanier Class 5 44667 out of Bradford past St Dunstans junction on 25th July 1967. *Photo: Peter Fitton*

BELOW: Only four months after construction, D1001 *Western Pathfinder* stands outside Swindon Works on 17th June 1962. It is in its original maroon livery with yellow buffer beams. *Photo: W. Potter*

Early Prototypes

LMS/English Electric Co 1,600hp Co-Co

After pioneering the development of the diesel locomotive for fifteen years with their 350/400 hp diesel shunters, the LMS was the first British company to introduce main line diesel electric traction in the form of two units, 10000 and 10001. 10000 was completed at Derby Works in early December 1947. After ten days of extensive tests and trial runs, it was despatched to London for inspection by the directors. Together with new Pacific 6256 it was on show at Euston on 18th December and subsequently took a test train to Watford and back.

The design of 10000 and 10001 had been the responsibility of Mr H G Ivatt, Chief Mechanical Engineer of the LMS. That company was responsible for the mechanical construction whilst the diesel engine and electrical equipment was supplied by the English Electric Company.

After completing extensive trials between Derby and Trent, 10000 entered regular traffic on 23rd February 1948 when it hauled the 8.55am Derby to St. Pancras, returning to Derby with the 2.15pm from St. Pancras. 10001 being completed six months after Nationalisation.

10000/10001 made their debut on the west coast main line on 7th October 1948 hauling the 11.40pm Euston to Glasgow sleeping car express as far as Carlisle. On 1st June 1949 they made a demonstration run with the down Royal Scot, arriving three minutes early at Glasgow Central and receiving the kind of welcome usually reserved for film stars, the crew posing for photographs and signing countless autograph books. However, steam traction made its reply when 46225 arrived at an adjacent platform also three minutes early, with the 10.10am ex Euston.

10000 was transferred to the Southern Region in March 1953, followed by 10001.

TOP: Six months before withdrawal, 10000 is climbing Camden bank with the 5.25pm Euston-Northampton local. A 4th June 1962 picture. *Photo: J.G. Dewing*

BOTTOM: Prior to its sale to the Brush Electric Engineering Co Ltd at Loughborough, 10800 was photographed at Derby on 7th August 1960. *Photo: W. Potter*

Initially, 10000 was kept to regular steam diagrams which included the 8.30am Waterloo to Bournemouth, returning at 1.05pm. Both 10000 and 10001 suffered failures on the Southern and were returned to the London Midland in April 1955.

During a visit to Derby Works in August 1956, 10000 was repainted in BR Brunswick green livery with the new British Railways emblem, the chromium numbers being painted over with cream paint. This livery was carried until another visit to Derby Works in September 1957 when it was outshopped in unlined green livery with the raised strake along the centre of the body picked out in aluminium. By October of that year 10001 had been similarly treated, but with white numerals and a pale green centre strake.

10000 was withdrawn from Willesden depot in December 1963, 10001 soldiering on in traffic until March 1966.

LMS/North British Loco Co 827hp Bo-Bo

As early as 1945, the LMS envisaged the construction of 10800, the last of three experimental designs for diesel electric traction. Whereas 10000/10001 were intended mainly for main-line passenger work, the 827 hp 10800 was designed for use on branch and cross country passenger and freight services, being of comparable capacity to the LMS 2-6-2T steam locomotives.

Built by the North British Locomotive Co, 10800 was delivered to Derby Works on 14th June 1950 and on 7th November made a demonstration run from Euston to Watford and back, meeting the schedule of 26 minutes with ease. From 8th to 11th November 10800 paid a visit to British Thompson-Houston Co Ltd, manufacturers of the four traction motors and electrical equipment, where a number of modifications and tests were effected.

10800 entered revenue earning service on 20th November 1950 when its diagram included service on the 6.18am Derby to Nottingham, 7.21am Nottingham to Kettering, returning from Nottingham to Derby at 1.08 pm. These diagrams continued in addition to workings to Manchester Central, until 4th January 1951 when the engine transferred to Bletchley for use on freight and mineral turns to Swanbourne, Ridgemont, Hinksey and Banbury.

In August 1952, 10800 was placed on loan to the Southern Region, being employed initially on the 10.45am London Bridge to Tunbridge Wells West via East Grinstead and the 1.08pm return. After use on a more intensive diagram it proved to be most inconsistent, and was repeatedly replaced by steam locomotives. In October 1952 it was ignominiously dismissed from passenger duties and relegated to goods trips from Norwood to Purley and Merstham. 10800 spent many months in shops, returning to its old haunts on 25th January 1954 when it hauled a trial 8 coach working from Brighton to East Croydon and back via Uckfield and Oxted. Once again 10800 returned to works. On 6th February 1954 it attempted to earn its living once more on local goods duties allocated to Norwood.

During a visit to Derby Works early in 1957, the engine emerged in green livery and was allocated to Rugby where it was employed on diagrams to Leicester.

In August 1959 it returned to Derby Works and was withdrawn from traffic, languishing until 1962 when it was sold to Brush Electric Engineering Co Ltd. Brush transformed it into a research locomotive named *Hawk*, intended for investigations into commutaterless traction motors. Eventually, lack of capital and the construction of HS4000 curtailed this experiment and apart from acting as a generator during the miners' strike of 1972, *Hawk* was cut up, some parts being stored.

SR/English Electric Co 1,750/2,000hp 1Co-Co1

Having invested heavily in main line electrification during the 1930s, the Southern Railway was always well advanced in terms of traction policies. O.V. Bulleid, the Southern's CME, aware that his lightweight Pacifics could be replaced by diesel-electric traction, was ahead of the LMS in approaching English Electric Co Ltd for a suitable power unit.

Due to the SR loading gauge and civil engineering restrictions, 10201 was built with a 1Co-Co1 wheel arrangement, i.e. one carrying axle and three motored axles on each bogie. The engine was similar to those fitted to 10000/10001, but developed 1,750 hp with a theoretical maximum speed of 110 mph. Roller bearings were fitted throughout, those on the driving axles being standard Timken boxes, whilst those on the radial axles

BELOW: Shortly after construction in March 1954, 10203 was being transferred to Willesden when it became derailed at Norwood Junction; this photograph shows re-railing activities *Photo: Colour-Rail/S.C. Townroe*

were cannon type boxes also being manufactured by Timken.

10201 underwent a series of trial runs between Ashford and Ramsgate before being painted at Ashford Works after Christmas 1950. 10202 was completed at Ashford in July 1950 and entered regular traffic on 25th September 1950 when it worked a regular diagram between Waterloo and Salisbury. A high speed test run followed on 24th October 1950 when 10202 took eight coaches from Salisbury to Waterloo. It had been the intention to maintain a 100 mph schedule over the racing ground between Hook and Fleet where special precautions had been taken to ensure a clear road for complete safety, but in the event speed was kept to a maximum of 87 mph due to the failure of 70004 during the previous week on the Eastern Section.

Trials of the new diesels on the SR's Eastern Section commenced on 8th February 1954 when 10202, on loan to Dover and manned by crews from that depot, worked a modified 430 duty, comprising the up Night Ferry, down and up Golden Arrows and down Night Ferry. These duties only lasted for a week before 10202 returned to Nine Elms.

The final locomotive in this group, 10203, emerged from Brighton Works on 7th March 1954, fitted with a modified version of the English Electric Co's engine giving a continuous traction rating of 2,000 hp.

10201/2 were transferred to the LMR in April 1955, 10201 working the down Mancunian (6pm ex-Euston) on 19th April 1955, 10203 following after some test runs on the Southern. This group of locomotives became the odd men out with regard to spare parts and servicing, all needing lengthy stays in Derby Works. 10201 and 10203 were stored at the end of 1962, 10202 following in spring 1963. All three were withdrawn at the end of 1963, final breaking taking place in 1968.

ABOVE: After withdrawal in December 1958, Fell 4-4-4-4DM is in the scrap line at Derby Works in April 1959. It was cut up in January 1960. *Photo: Colour-Rail/T.B. Owen*

BR/Paxman/Fell 2,040hp DM 2-D-2

Outshopped from Derby Works in May 1952, 10100 had been under construction since June 1949. This 4-4-4-4 locomotive was built to the system invented by Lt.-Col. L.F.R. Fell and developed by H.G. Ivatt and Fell Developments Ltd. Originally, power was to have been provided by four 500 hp Ricardo engines, but during construction the decision was taken to install four Davey-Paxman 12-cylinder diesel engines giving a continuously rated 2,000 hp; two at each of the outer ends of the locomotive. The mechanical transmission comprised fluid couplings with gearing incorporated into the drive, and was designed to give a progressively changing speed ratio in order to approach the performance and flexibility of a steam engine without the difficulties then experienced with diesel power through electrical transmission.

The 4ft 3in coupled wheels were driven through gearing calculated to give the locomotive a top speed of 78 mph when the four main engines were running at their maximum speed of 1,500 rpm.

10100 made its public debut at Marylebone station on 23rd May 1951, towed by brand new BR Standard Class 4 75000. This was followed by a succession of test runs on the Midland main line; some to St Pancras and others to Manchester Central via Chinley. One run on 12th September 1951 resulted in a failure at Glendon when single line working had to be introduced for two hours before 10100 could be removed.

10100 went into regular traffic on 21st January 1952, its duties including the 7.10am to Manchester Central slow, arriving at 10.50am and returning with the 11.35am semi-fast. After a period on the Midland lines, 10100 was used for acceleration trials on the Cheshire Lines between Manchester Central and Liverpool Central. Prior to these tests a number of alterations to lineside structures had been made for clearance purposes. After returning to its Manchester-St Pancras duties for a brief spell in 1954, 10100 commenced trials on the Settle and Carlisle line on April 25th 1955 with a dynamometer car and mobile test unit.

Between workings, 10100 spent much time languishing in Derby Works and on one visit in March 1957, 10100 was repainted in green livery with the new BR emblem.

10100's chequered career came to an end at Manchester Central on 16th October 1958 when an oil fire broke out while it was waiting to take out the 12.25pm to Derby. The Manchester fire brigade were summoned but luckily no one was hurt. By December 1958, 10100 had been returned to Derby shed where it was dumped near the coaling plant and after a period in store in the works was scrapped in July 1960.

English Electric Co 'Deltic' 3,300hp Co-Co

As early as December 1954, English Electric had decided to invest in the construction of their 3,300 hp prototype locomotive, *Deltic*. After success with the Napier-Deltic diesel engine in marine applications, EE planned a powerful express locomotive to meet BR needs with the added possibility of export sales. The two lightweight Napier engines were accommodated in a structure which weighed 32 tons less than the later 2,500 hp Peaks, *Deltic* having the benefit of an extra 800 hp.

With export potential in mind, the livery was American style — blue with yellow stripes with a non-functional headlight at each end. *Deltic* was completed in October 1955 and worked various trial trips from Speke Junction. On 13th December 1955, it appeared for the first time on a passenger train, working from Edge Hill shed on one of the regular Pacific turns, the 10.10am Merseyside Express from Liverpool Lime Street to London Euston, returning with the Shamrock at 4.55pm (SX) the same afternoon. On its return it arrived on time at Lime Street in spite of delays.

With the pending electrification of the LMR's west coast main line, *Deltic's* future obviously lay elsewhere and it was transferred to York on 13th January 1956 for trials on the NER. After two days of tests it ventured as far as Marshalls Meadow (Berwick) with a six-wheeled saloon on 16th January. It proved to be slightly out of gauge, losing its cab steps at Darlington and dislodging a section of platform edge at Newcastle (Manors). By the end of that month it had been transferred to Hornsey for trials on the GNR. Unfortunately it failed on arrival and was returned to works for a replacement No. 1 power unit. Non-stop trials between Kings Cross and Newcastle commenced on 16th March 1959 when Deltic hauled dynamometer car DB 999500 and empty coaching stock. This run terminated at Gateshead (Greenfield) due to the limited clearances at Newcastle Central. The journey was completed in 3 hours 45 minutes, some 15 minutes faster than the pre-war Silver Jubilee timing.

The undoubted success of the prototype *Deltic* resulted in an order being placed for 22 similar machines in 1958, to replace 55 ex-LNER Pacifics on the east coast main line. After a failure at Doncaster in 1961, *Deltic* was returned to the English Electric company, where after many attempts at export sales it was restored to pristine condition at their Vulcan foundry, prior to presentation to the Science Museum in Kensington where it remains as a permanent exhibit.

BELOW: English Electric prototype *Deltic* is rounding Gamston curve with a Leeds-Kings Cross express in October 1958. *Photo: K.R. Pirt/K.R. Photographics*

ABOVE: Pilot scheme English-Electric Type A, D8002 passes over Castlethorpe troughs with an up local in May 1958. *Photo: Colour-Rail/T.B. Owen*

BELOW: Sister engine, D8015 is portrayed outside Willesden motive power depot on 15th March 1959 alongside 4F 44242. *Photo: W. Potter*

Pilot Schemes

English Electric Co 1,000hp Bo-Bo Type A(1)

Of all the locomotives delivered under BR's pilot schemes, the D8000 class has outlived most of its contemporaries. The success of these 1,000 hp Bo-Bo's lay with the design, which incorporated well proven equipment. Considerable effort was also made to produce an attractive piece of industrial design. The first of the class, D8000, was formally handed over by the English Electric company to the BTC on 3rd June 1957.

The first twenty of the class were allocated to Devons Road motive power depot, the first steam depot in the country to be completely converted for the maintenance of diesel locomotives. However, the life of Devons Road was to be relatively short; closed from 10th February 1964, its duties were divided between Stratford and Willesden. The 1,000 hp locomotives allocated to Devons Road were fitted with ATC equipment and on 2nd January 1958, D8014 was used to conduct signalling tests between Waterloo and Farnborough in order to test AWS equipment which had been installed on certain sections of the Central Section main line. One problem observed on this run was the poor visibility when running bonnet first. Because of visibility problems with the D8000, D8200 and D8400 classes, BR decided that all future diesel electric locomotives in this power range would be built to a new Bo-Bo design incorporating two Davey Paxman engines which were to be placed on each side of a full width central driving cab. An initial order for 88 for use on the Scottish Region were placed with the Clayton Equipment Co of Hatton, Derby.

Not all BR type 1s were built to the same design, D8000-D8127 being fitted with disc train reporting equipment whilst D8128-D8327 were fitted with four character route indicators. Some of the class were not constructed at Vulcan, D8020-D8034 and D8050-D8127 being built by R.S.H. Limited.

With a service availability approaching 90% the D8000 class (now BR Class 20) have the acclaim of their drivers and maintenance men with no fewer than 176 still being in use at May 1988.

Brush Traction Co 1,250/1,365/1,600/2,000hp A1A-A1A Type B(2/3/4)

Designated to be the diesel mixed-traffic equivalent of the LNER B1 4-6-0s and the LMSR Class 5s, the first of the pilot scheme Type Bs (later Type 2), D5500, was handed over to the BTC at a ceremony at the Brush locomotive works on 31st October 1957. After trials between Loughborough and Chinley it was delivered to the Great Eastern section of the ER, making its first journey in revenue earning service on 13th November 1957 on the 10.36am Liverpool Street to Clacton. Prior to this working, crew training had been conducted between Shenfield and Southend (Victoria), involving hauling 25 empty wagons between these points, the time allowed being 48 minutes. Similar workings with eight coaches were allowed 37 minutes.

The class's normal green livery blended into the general backcloth of the countryside and with their relatively quiet operation, the engines were a danger to permanent way staff, several being killed on the ER. In an effort to overcome this problem the ER authorised two locomotives to be painted in more visible experimental liveries, D5578 being outshopped in chromatic blue and D5579 in golden ochre. The widespread introduction of yellow warning panels was yet to come.

Following the success of the twenty pilot scheme locomotives, the BTC authorised an order for a further 243 engines, to be constructed in various batches, many of these are still active today. After original orders for the ER, the fleet has operated all over BR.

TOP: The production batches of Brush Type 2s were basically similar to the pilot scheme design, although the introduction of a four panel route indicator altered their front end appearance. The two variations are depicted here at Stratford mpd on 27th February 1960. The locomotive on the left is carrying the experimental golden ochre livery and D5545 in green livery stands alongside. *Photo: M.S. Welch*

BOTTOM: Production version, D5679 passes Belle Isle with an up local for Kings Cross. An 18th March 1961 picture. *Photo: R.C. Riley*

English Electric Co 2,000hp 1Co-Co1 Type C(4)

Built as part of the 1955 Modernisation Plan, the first of the ten pilot scheme English Electric Type Cs (later type 4s), D200, travelled from the Vulcan Foundry at Newton le Willows to Doncaster Works for acceptance trials on 14th March 1958. The first of these took place on 19th March when D200 worked a down e.c.s. special which followed in the path of the 10.10am Kings Cross to Aberdeen. It worked several more trials, including some on the GE from Stratford to Cambridge in April. Its 'public' debut came on 18th April when it worked a nine coach train from Liverpool Street to Norwich with roof boards announcing "The first 2,000 hp diesel run between Norwich and Liverpool St" and "Progress on the Great Eastern".

The allocation of the first batch of ten locomotives was shared between Stratford for GE line duties and Hornsey where their GN line activities included use on the Flying Scotsman, Master Cutler and Tees Tyne Pullman, D209 was the first member of the class to haul the Flying Scotsman, on 31st January 1959. A spate of failures dogged the class at that time including many problems with the train heating boilers.

Production of the class resumed in May 1959 when a further six batches were constructed bringing the total number of the class in traffic to two hundred. The first of the production batch, D211, had the distinction of being the first member of the class to arrive in Glasgow when it worked the 4.15pm Crewe to Glasgow Central on 19th August 1960.

The EE Type 4s had their share of the headlines. On 7th August 1961, D249 on an up freight overran the up refuge loop at Grantshouse, ran through the goods shed and demolished many of the station buildings on the up side. On 21st April 1963 D216 was hauling the 12.20pm from Holyhead to Euston at Kings Langley when it struck a crane which was working at an adjacent platform. D216 suffered considerable damage at the front end, but the train, which was travelling at reduced speed, escaped lightly, only the first four of its fourteen vehicles being derailed.

Without doubt the single most publicised event which affected any British diesel locomotive happened on 8th August 1963. D326 was hauling the 6.50pm Glasgow to Euston mail train when it was halted by signals at Sears Crossing, north of Cheddington. A masked gang had tampered with the colour light signals and then proceeded to rob the train of an estimated £2,500,000 in registered mail, bank notes and

jewellery. This was not the only event to befall D326; on 4th August 1965 it was stabled in a siding near Winson Green with no crew on board when it careered off in the direction of Birmingham New Street. At Monument Lane it crashed into a permanent way train and was derailed, to be towed away to Crewe on 17th August for major repairs.

This class was one of the most successful of the pilot scheme types, some examples soldiering on in traffic for over 25 years.

LEFT, TOP: Delivered to the GE in July 1958, D205 is climbing Bethnal Green bank with the 12.30pm Liverpool St-Norwich on 28th February 1959. Members of this class remained on the GE until January 1965, when they were displaced by the Brush/Sulzer 2,750hp Type 4s. *Photo: R.C. Riley*

LEFT, BOTTOM: After arriving from the Vulcan Foundry at Newton-le-Willows, D205 is awaiting acceptance trials at Doncaster Works on 13th July 1958. *Photo: W. Potter*

ABOVE: Prior to the introduction of yellow warning panels, EE Type 4 D268 is taking water from Bushey troughs whilst working the up Shamrock on 7th May 1960. This operation replenished the water in the locomotive's train heating boiler. *Photo: T.B. Owen*

British Thomson-Houston 800hp Bo-Bo Type A(1)

Intended primarily for use on main line and cross country freight working, D8200 and its nine pilot scheme sisters were initially allocated to Devons Road motive power depot. Having travelled from the builders, Yorkshire Engine Company, BTC received D8200 at a ceremony at Euston station on 18th November 1957. All ten members of the initial order were subjected to extensive trials over the Settle and Carlisle route prior to delivery, most workings with eleven coaches from Sheffield Wincobank down sidings to Appleby and return.

Constructed for operation in multiples of up to three, the locomotives had no steam heating, although a 'through' pipe was fitted so that they could be coupled inside as a booster to other locomotive types with steam heating. However, this did not preclude their use on summertime excursions from east London to the south coast.

The overall appearance of the class was pleasing, the design being the work of consultant designers Allen Barnes, Bowden Ltd whom the BTC had engaged. A follow-on order for 34 was constructed by BTH which eventually led to a total of 44. They were not notably successful, suffering from frequent engine problems, mainly due to piston seizures with resultant extensive maintenance.

BR policies eventually effected the future of this class, wagon load freight proving increasingly uneconomical and this, coupled with the fact that they could not be employed on passenger work in the winter months, led to their early withdrawal, beginning in 1968, the class becoming extinct in March 1971.

ABOVE: After one year in traffic, D8202 is portrayed outside Willesden mpd on 15th March 1959. *Photo: W. Potter*

North British Loco 800hp Bo-Bo Type A(1)

The design of the ten pilot scheme Type A (later Type 1) 800 hp locomotives, D8400-9, built by the North British Locomotive Company, closely resembled the stark appearance of the pioneer LMSR Bo-Bo 10800 which NBL had built in 1950. Outwardly, they were box like and austere, although some effort had been made to improve the design of the cab by placing the doors in the side instead of at the ends.

All ten locomotives were allocated to Stratford motive power depot where they were used on freight traffic, including inter-regional workings to Hither Green and New Cross Gate, and parcels traffic between Liverpool Street and Southend.

As with the D8200 class locomotives, the power units suffered piston seizures, a problem attributed to inadequate engine ventilation, and were also liable to pyrotechnic displays with the resultant disruption to services.

Sensibly, no further locomotives of this class were ordered, and after a somewhat shortlived and chequered career, they were quietly withdrawn from service in 1968, only ten years after construction.

ABOVE: Prior to delivery to the GE, D8401 is awaiting acceptance trials at Doncaster Works on 13th July 1958. *Photo: W. Potter*

ABOVE: Its original wrapround cab windows replaced with smaller panes of glass, D5714 is passing Carnforth with the 18.50 Heysham Moss to Whitehaven Fina tank train. A 5th June 1964 picture. *Photo: D.A. Codling*

BELOW: D5717 is in original condition outside Cricklewood mpd on 4th October 1959: wrapround cab windows and no yellow panels. *Photo: W. Potter*

Metropolitan-Vickers 1,200hp Co-Bo Type B(2)

Even to the most broad-minded observer of new diesel locomotives, the appearance of the 1,200 hp Metropolitan-Vickers Co-Bos must have been distinctly odd, with their different bogies, one six wheel and one four wheel, and unusual livery scheme, various parts being picked out in duckegg blue. They also had wrap-around cab front windows, no cab side windows, and one cab door positioned well to the rear of the cab on the driver's side at each end.

These machines commenced trial working on 7th July 1958, D5700 taking a fourteen coach test train from Metropolitan-Vickers works at Bowsfield, Stockton, to Leeds. Trouble was experienced and several unscheduled stops had to be made, resulting in a 90 minute late arrival on the return journey.

D5700/1 hauled a special test train which consisted of 25 fitted 'Platefits' loaded with 50 containers on 1st October 1958 from Hendon to Gushetfaulds Goods via Leicester, Sheffield, Leeds, Carlisle, Beattock, Carstairs and Motherwell. The inaugural run of the London to Glasgow Condor freight took place on 16th March 1959, the main attraction to potential customers being that the containers were collected in the late afternoon with a guaranteed delivery in Glasgow the following morning at a cost of £16 for a small container and £18 for a large container.

By November 1959 demand for this service was flagging, some workings consisting of only 13 wagons and one engine. As a result of locomotive problems, by 4th January 1960 no fewer than 17 out of 20 were stopped for repairs at Cricklewood, their duties on the Condor being performed by Stanier Class 5s. In July 1962 the Condor was back up to its full load, then entrusted to Type 4s, the Co-Bos having been returned to the Metropolitan-Vickers works at Dukinfield for modification and overhaul. Following this they were reallocated to Barrow, ending their days on local passenger and freight duties, the class being withdrawn by 1968, just ten years old.

Of the twenty members of this class only one, D5701, came to be outshopped in BR blue. D5705 was used after withdrawal by the RTC at Derby, and subsequently secured for preservation.

ABOVE: Newly constructed BR/Sulzer Type B D5020 is portrayed outside the test house at Derby Works in October 1959. *Photo: Raymond Reed*

BELOW: The final development of the BR/Sulzer Bo-Bo had a complete re-design of the bodywork. The gangway doors were omitted and the air intake grills were sited in the roof; the whole appearance was enhanced by two-tone green livery. D5282 stands outside Derby mpd on 28th June 1964. *Photo: T.B. Owen*

British Railways/Sulzer 1,160/1,250hp Bo-Bo Type B(2)

Constructed at BR's Derby Works as No. 1 in main line diesel order B251, D5000 travelled to Marylebone for inspection by Sir Brian Robertson, chairman of the BTC, on 24th July 1958. The first five members of this class were powered by Sulzer engines built in Switzerland, other engines being built under licence by Vickers Armstrong of Barrow. The class were designed to a loading gauge of 12ft 8in, this allowing their use over the widened lines of the London Transport Executive.

D5000 commenced its revenue earning service on 15th September 1958, when it worked the 9.38am Derby to Manchester, 12.30pm Manchester to Liverpool Central, returning on the 2.30pm from Liverpool Central to Derby.

By late January 1959, D5000 was the first of fifteen members of the class to be loaned to the Southern Region, where it was used for crew training between Ashford and Faversham. Each locomotive weighed some five tons more than expected, and the civil engineer vetoed their use on certain sections. In order to overcome this problem, some locomotives had their train heating boilers removed. This meant that there became two distinct groups of locomotives, D5002-6 and D5000/1/7-14, the latter having greater freedom of route availability.

The weight of most of the early diesels gave rise to another problem, the lack of braking force capability. This became obvious on 10th November 1959; D5000, hauling a coal train from Snowdown Colliery, ran through Snowdown station out of control, ploughed through a sand drag, demolished buffer stops, and finally came to rest on the side of a low cutting, fouling the up main line. With similar problems on other regions, a number of special 'diesel brake tenders' were constructed to give added braking power.

Eventually a total of 477 BR/Sulzer Type 2 locomotives were constructed, D7667 holding the honour of being the 1000th diesel locomotive to be built at Derby. The first 151 members of this class were later designated BR Class 24, the remainder, having an up-rated 1,250hp Sulzer engine and redesigned body, becoming Class 25.

The two classes gave sterling service in traffic, the final members of Class 25 being withdrawn in 1987.

Birmingham Railway Carriage & Wagon Co 1,160/1,250hp Bo-Bo Type B(2)

Built by the Birmingham Railway Carriage and Wagon Company, the twenty pilot scheme Bo-Bo 1,160 hp locomotives were initially allocated to Hornsey (34B) mpd. Fitted with Sulzer engines and Crompton Parkinson traction equipment, they were intended to replace the ageing N2 0-6-2Ts, primarily on the outer suburban services to Hitchin and Hertford North.

Initially delivered to Doncaster Works, D5300 was observed working to Barkston on acceptance trials on 6th August 1958, prior to travelling to Hornsey where it was used for crew training. It was found that there was only limited use for these machines on suburban duties and D5303 was despatched to Aberdeen where it was tried out on workings to Inverness and Glasgow. Such was its success that the other nineteen pilot scheme locomotives were soon to follow.

There were some initial problems with the engines but after considerable modification, the general design proved to be most satisfactory, the BTC eventually ordering a total of 116 machines. In September 1961, new locomotives D5347/8 were successfully tried out on the West Highland line, D5348 being stationed at Stirling where it underwent tests on the Callander and Oban line, replacing two of the temperamental D61XX machines.

By April 1966, the pilot scheme batch was beginning to give problems, especially over the Waverley route. This resulted in some of the class being fitted for slow-speed running to work merry go round coal traffic to Cockenzie power station. It was at this time that the corridor connections were sealed out of use and two cylindrical air tanks fitted, these being visible below the bodywork.

This group of locomotives were later formed into two classes, BR Class 26 and Class 27. Whilst there were a number of technical modifications built into the class 27s, they were visually distinguishable by their four-panel headcode box, the Class 26 having disc route indicators. The refurbished Class 26s continue in service but all Class 27s were withdrawn in 1987.

ABOVE: Production version BRCW Type 2, D5368, is arriving at Spean Bridge station on 6th July 1965 with the 7.48am Mallaig to Glasgow Queen Street. Basically similar to the pilot scheme locomotives, the Scottish Regions engines' modifications included a recess for the single line tablet catcher and sliding cabside windows. *Photo: M. Mensing*

British Railways/Sulzer 'Peaks' 2,300/2,500hp 1Co-Co1 Type C(4)

Ordered as part of the 1955 Modernisation Plan and constructed under BR's 1959 locomotive building programme, D1, the first of the ten pilot scheme Peaks, emerged from Derby Works in April 1959. It travelled up to London for inspection on 21st April and was officially named *Scafell Pike* by Sir Fergus Graham, Lord Lieutenant of Cumberland, during a ceremony at Carlisle Citadel station on 14th July 1959.

The ten 2,300 hp pilot scheme locomotives were designated Class ML4, being initially allocated to Crewe for use on mixed traffic duties between Euston and Glasgow. The BTC placed orders for a further 183 members of this class which were equipped with more powerful 2,500 hp engines. The pilot scheme engines were later designated as Class 44 and, being somewhat non-standard, were eventually concentrated at Toton where they were used on freight in the Midlands. Under the BR reclassification scheme, D11-D137 became 45.001-45.077 and 45.101 to 45.150, whilst the Brush-equipped locomotives became 46.001-46.056 of Class 46.

The Peaks will always be associated with their duties on the Midland main line. The dieselisation of the Manchester services was virtually complete by February 1961 and led to a marked improvement in timekeeping. The class were regular performers on the cross-country services from north-east to south-west, being the first diesel-electrics to be received by the WR, penetrating the diesel-hydraulic strongholds of Devon and Cornwall and dominating these duties for many years until the introduction of the InterCity 125 units in 1983.

Whilst two of the pilot scheme locos, 44.044/8, are secure in preservation, the last of the Class 45s were scheduled for withdrawal in May 1988.

OPPOSITE: Derby designed Sulzer powered Peak D97 outside Crewe Works on 16th April 1961. The twin indicator boxes replaced the disc and electric light headcodes. *Photo: W. Potter*

LEFT: Pilot scheme Type 4 Peak, D4 *Great Gable* had its train heating boiler replenished at Rugby Midland station whilst working the 8.20am Carlisle to Euston express on 23rd December 1961. *Photo: J.N. Simms*

BELOW: BR/Sulzer production series 2,500hp Peak D154 heads an up unfitted coal freight south of Duffield station on 30th April 1966. *Photo: M. Mensing*

North British Loco Co 1,000/1,100hp Bo-Bo Type B(2)

The first of the North British Locomotive Co 1000 hp diesel-electrics left Queens Park works on 5th December 1958. Subsequent trials with an eight coach train took place on both 8th and 12th December, on the latter occasion the whole ensemble having to be hauled back to the works by a J11. The first batch of ten locomotives (D6100-9) were built as part of BR's pilot scheme and were initially allocated to Hornsey for use on GN line suburban duties.

Prior to reallocation of the whole class to the Scottish Region, D6130 made a trial trip over the West Highland on 12th November 1959, working the 6.45am Glasgow to Mallaig. Progress was lamentable, Mallaig being reached some eighty minutes late with subsequent delays to the MacBraynes steamers. On the return journey, D6130 made even worse progress, arriving in Glasgow some two and a half hours late, the official explanation being "it couldn't take to the hills", although a more likely reason was that the sanding gear had been defective on a day of heavy rain — a phenomena not unknown on the West Highland. However, D6130 managed to redeem itself on 14th January 1960 when it made a successful trip on the Oban road, working the 7.55am from Glasgow, gaining some twenty one minutes with a four coach load. Meanwhile, sister engines D6100-9 had been placed in store at Peterborough whilst a decision was made about their future use.

After reallocation to Scotland, various members of this class were prone to pyrotechnic displays. On 29th March 1962 D6127 caught fire whilst working in multiple on the 3.15pm Glasgow Buchanan Street to Dundee at Greenloaning, little above the bogies and frames being left intact.

In February 1962 a proposal was made to downgrade the D6100-37 series to Type 1s and rebuild them to resemble in outline the D8000 series, thus improving all-round visibility and fitting them for freight work where their vagaries would be more acceptable. D6130 probably entered Queens Park Works to estimate with such modification in mind, but was later sent out when closure of the works was announced on 3rd April 1962.

Due to the problems with the NBL/MAN L12V18/21 power units, 20 of the fleet were re-engined in 1965 with Paxman 12YJXL units in an attempt to improve availability. Original locomotives became Class 21, re-engined examples becoming Class 29.

By December 1967 many of the class had been placed in store, the last members disappearing in December 1971.

ABOVE: After working acceptance trials from Doncaster, production series NBL Type 2 D6114 is pictured outside Stratford Works on 2nd June 1959. *Photo: R.C. Riley*

BELOW: NBL Type 2 D6152 leaves Stonehaven with a local for Aberdeen. A May 1965 picture. *Photo: K.R. Pirt/K.R. Photographics*

English Electric Co 'Baby Deltics' 1,110hp Bo-Bo Type B(2)

Following problems with the D5300 Sulzer engined diesels which were prohibited from working over the LT Widened Lines to the Southern Region (due to their axle loading being in excess of the load stipulated by the DCE), the Eastern Region had similar troubles with the D5900 series from English Electric, D5900 being rejected by BR whilst at the builders until its weight was reduced. This required modifications to the superstructure, bogies and many other components including the fitting of lightweight Oleo Pneumatic buffers.

After tests were conducted on 12th February 1960 when D5903/5 worked in multiple on a coal train from Whitemoor to Bury St Edmunds, it was planned to allocate the class to the Sheffield area for use on colliery work, a proposal that was never implemented. Instead, the class was transferred to Finsbury Park, partly eliminating steam traction from suburban passenger and empty stock duties.

By late April 1962, the availability of Baby Deltics had reached a low ebb, only two being in traffic. As each engine failed, it was withdrawn from traffic and stored, pending return to English Electric where an extensive refurbishing programme was put in hand.

The first locomotive to return to traffic was D5905 in June 1964, a Finsbury Park engine. Major improvements included the removal of gangway doors and headcode discs, and this, in conjunction with a new four panel route indicator, looked considerably neater.

Failures continued, however, and despite the extensive modifications, the class did not escape BR's rationalisation plan, the last member, D5909, being withdrawn in March 1971. D5905 was retained by the Research Division at Derby, operating various test trains until November 1975.

TOP: Prior to delivery to Hornsey mpd (34B), newly constructed 'Baby Deltics' D5905/6 are lined up at Doncaster Works awaiting acceptance trials on 10th May 1959. *Photo: W. Potter*

ABOVE: 'Baby Deltic' D5906 is pictured between the tunnels at Kings Cross with a Cambridge service on 18th May 1961. *Photo: R.C. Riley*

ABOVE: After ten months in traffic, NBL A1A-A1A D602 *Bulldog* rests outside Swindon shed on 20th September 1959. *Photo: W. Potter*

BELOW: On home territory, D602 is working an up express of chocolate and cream stock across Largin viaduct. A July 1959 picture. *Photo: Colour-Rail/B.J. Swain*

WR Hydraulics

North British Loco Co 2,000hp A1A-A1A

Ordered in September 1955 as Swindon Lot No 425, the five North British diesel-hydraulic locomotives, D600-D604 were constructed for the Western Region as part of BR's 1958 locomotive construction programme. The first, D600, commenced trials in Scotland in November 1957 prior to travelling to Swindon on 13th January 1958. By the end of January, it had received the name *Active, Warship Class* on one side only when it was posed for official photographs to be taken. The initial livery applied to this batch of locomotives was an overall Brunswick green with a single blue-grey line between the cab doors along the body side.

On 17th February 1958, D600 was employed on a special nine-coach demonstration run from Paddington to Bristol when it attained speeds of over 90 mph. On the return journey, one of the two 1,000 hp engines failed near Badminton, the remainder of the journey being completed on one engine, arrival back at Paddington being some nineteen minutes late.

After working a special to Newton Abbot on 19th April 1958, D600 commenced revenue earning service two days later on a double return daily trip between Penzance and Plymouth which included the 'Limited' in both directions.

These original pilot scheme Type C diesel-hydraulics were intended for both express passenger and freight, but the lighter weight of the diesel-hydraulics compared to the diesel-electrics rendered them less effective on freight haulage.

With the introduction of the D800 class, the A1A-A1As were displaced from their principal duties on the West of England main line and relegated to work on Cornish china clay traffic. Apart from an initial allocation to Swindon, the class spent the whole of its working life allocated to Plymouth Laira until August 1967 when D601/2/4 were transferred to Landore. Whilst at Landore, these locos also worked from Margam and Pantyffynon, where instructors were provided. Due to their unsuitability on the South Wales main line the trio were returned to Laira and in December 1967 placed in store with others of the class. The end came for D600/1 on 22nd July 1968 when they were towed to Woodham's Yard, Barry, followed by D604/3/2 on 29th July.

BR Swindon/North British 2,100/2,200hp B-B

D800 was the first main line diesel locomotive to be built by BR at Swindon and was completed in July 1958. Its design followed closely that of the Deutsche Bundesbahn V200 series, which incorporated the use of a stressed skin construction enabling a high power to weight ratio to be achieved.

The first of the Swindon built 2,200 hp locomotives, D800, was named *Sir Brian Robertson* at a ceremony at Paddington on 14th July 1958. Attending the ceremony were Mr R Hanks, Chairman of the Western Area Board and other officials, the naming being carried out by Mr K W C Grand. Having arrived from Swindon earlier in the day, D800 worked a press trip after the ceremony. The train of four chocolate and cream coaches travelled to Reading and back. Entering traffic the following day, D800 took the down Cornish Riviera from Paddington to Plymouth, returning with the 4.10pm from Plymouth.

The first three locomotives of this class were a belated addition to BR's pilot scheme orders; and whilst the design was almost entirely due to German engineering skill, D800 was constructed almost entirely by hand, the staff at Swindon having to translate specifications into a design that would fit the British loading gauge. Whilst the 33 and the final five locomotives in this class were constructed at Swindon, D833-D865 were

BELOW: Three years after their introduction on the Torbay Express, D842 *Royal Oak* passes Saltern Cove on 8th August 1962. *Photo: W. Potter*

built by NBL in Glasgow. After the first batch entered traffic, WR drivers experienced rough riding whenever speeds in excess of 75 mph were attained. This problem was attributed to the bogie design and after tests in 1959/60 modifications were introduced which successfully overcame it.

On 27th July 1959, D807 *Caradoc* had the honour of being the first diesel to haul the up Torbay Express. During the previous week 5008 *Raglan Castle* and 5032 *Usk Castle* had been the regular performers. The introduction of diesel power to this working led to the schedule of the down working being cut by ten minutes to 165 min between London and Exeter, this being the fastest time ever recorded between these cities.

Apart from the bogie troubles, the D800s gave the WR excellent service with top speeds in excess of the authorised 90mph. Under BR's rationalisation policy which began in 1968, withdrawal of this class commenced and all 71 engines had disappeared by the end of 1972.

ABOVE: Carrying the later maroon livery, D863 *Warrior* heads an up freight past Didcot on 19th March 1966. *Photo: W.A. Kelsey*

RIGHT: Resplendent in its original colour scheme, D870 *Zulu* marshals parcels vans at Reading in April 1961. *Photo: H.G. Forsythe*

LEFT: Waiting for the road at Exeter St Davids, D804 *Avenger* heads a train of Presflo cement wagons on 16th August 1967. *Photo: H.W. Bolton*

BELOW: Doyen of the class, D800 *Sir Brian Robertson*, approaches Vauxhall on a Waterloo to West of England express. An October 1966 picture. *Photo: Raymond Reed*

North British Loco Co 1,000/1,100hp B-B

Ordered as part of BR's 1955 Modernisation Plan, the first six members of this class featured the same general configuration as their sister D6100 locomotives which had been ordered for the ER from the North British Locomotive Company. However, the D6300 class employed a Voith hydraulic transmission, so that comparisons could be made between similar machines with both hydraulic and electric transmissions.

These locomotives were part of a plan to eliminate steam traction between Newton Abbot and Penzance, to be achieved with the introduction of approximately 130 diesel-hydraulic locomotives displacing an estimated 200 steam engines. After weighing and testing at Swindon, the first of the class, D6300, entered traffic on 12th January 1959 when it took the 7.35am from Swindon to Bristol and continued to work on local trips in the Bristol area for a further three weeks.

Initially allocated to Plymouth Laira motive power depot for use in Devon and Cornwall, the D63XXs, on the main line, were invariably used in pairs. Contemporary reports suggested that there were insufficient trains capable of being worked by a single engine, but in practice the use of two locomotives in tandem was preferred in case of failure in one engine, when the other could take the train forward and not block the main line.

The class, which eventually ran to 58 members, was more at home on secondary duties and local freight work, but with the closure of so many branch lines in the West Country, they became too numerous to retain in one area and were later to be seen all over the WR territory, one of their final duties being the empty stock workings between Paddington and Old Oak Common.

ABOVE: Carrying the same style of livery as the larger D600s, newly delivered NBL B-B D6329 is at Laira motive power depot on 27th June 1960. This picture shows the unusual sideways-folding headcode discs and simplified front end detail. Incorporating a gangway for multiple unit operation, the front end resembled the NBL Warship A1A-A1A, minus the nose. *Photo: W. Potter*

ABOVE: 1,000 hp B-B D6335 leaves Kingswear with an up working on 8th August 1962. At that time Dartmouth was being used for the start of The Tall Ships Race, the sail training ship *Amerigo Vespucci* being moored in the background. *Photo: W. Potter*

Beyer Peacock (Hymek) Ltd 1,700hp B-B

The first of the 101 Beyer-Peacock 1700 hp Class ML3 (later Type 3) locomotives was handed over to BR's Western Region officials at a ceremony at Paddington on 16th May 1961. Equipped with a single Bristol-Siddeley Maybach MD870 engine, the class had a maximum permitted working speed of 90 mph. An initial attractive appearance was achieved by using blending shades of green livery with ivory white cab surrounds and raised metal numbers. Being designed to operate in multiples of up to three locomotives, it was not possible for them to work in conjunction with any other class.

Entering revenue earning service in the week commencing 10th July 1961, their initial duties were in the Bristol area. By October of that year, sufficient experience had been gained with this class for D7023/4 to be entrusted to Royal Train duty when they were used to convey a royal party from Paddington to the new steel works at Llanwern where a short platform and canopy had been erected. Notable guests taking part in this ceremony were conveyed in two separate trains hauled by 6000 *King George V* and 6018 *King Henry VI*, the latter carrying a 'R.T.B. Spencer Works' headboard.

Such was the BTC's haste to introduce dieselisation in 1959, that 45 locomotives of this class were ordered without a single prototype being constructed. At that time it was envisaged that a further 200 locomotives of this class would be constructed, but subsequent orders gave a fleet total of 101. With BR deciding against the use of diesel-hydraulic locomotives, preference was given to the construction of further diesel-electrics.

Operating on numerous cross-country routes, the 'Hymeks' fulfilled their role, handling many of the duties formerly entrusted to the GWR Castles, but their demise began with the introduction of BR's Rationalisation Policy, many of the class being withdrawn in 1972, although a few survivors lingered on in traffic until 1975.

TOP: Recently delivered from the Gorton Works of Beyer Peacock, D7000 stands outside Swindon Works in May 1961. *Photo: Colour-Rail/N. Browne*

BOTTOM: Working the 12.25pm Gloucester-Swindon local, Beyer Peacock (Hymek) D7088 stops at Brimscombe, 2-6-2T 6106 stands outside the shed between banking duties. A 26th September 1964 picture. *Photo: W. Potter*

BELOW: Photographed at Norton Junction, east of Worcester, 1,700hp B-B D7063 is working the 11.15am Paddington to Hereford. From D7003 onwards the twin air horns were located on the cab roof. *Photo: M. Mensing*

BR Swindon/Crewe 2,700hp C-C

Constructed as a replacement for the WR's King class, the first of the C-C 2,700 hp Western class diesel-hydraulics, D1000 *Western Enterprise* commenced trials from Swindon in February 1962. D1000 was outshopped in an experimental desert sand livery, the subsequent engine, D1001 *Western Pathfinder*, being finished in an overall maroon livery with yellow bufferbeams. After using these two liveries the WR was undecided on an appropriate livery for the remaining members of the class and organised a competition amongst junior enthusiasts, the prize being a free trip on one of the locomotives. The winning entry chose maroon livery, although one entry suggested that *Devon* Sand would be appropriate; her address — Newton Abbot.

As with the WR's Hymeks, the BTC did not construct a prototype, no fewer than 74 locomotives being ordered in October 1959. It was intended that 35 be constructed at Swindon with 39 at Crewe, but Crewe also constructed the last five of Swindon's allocation. As with the D800's, the basic design of the Westerns was of German origin, the bodywork again being of the stressed-skin steel construction.

With the introduction of this class, passed for 90 mph running, many of the WR's principal services were accelerated, one example being the South Wales Pullman which had its journey time reduced by 15 minutes. One major change to this class commenced in August 1968 when D1066 was fitted with air-brakes. This was achieved by a reduction in the fuel tank at one end of the centre skirt, a large compressor being fitted transversely into this space.

During their lifetime the Westerns slowly achieved a cult following, with many enthusiasts following their last workings in 1977. Such was their popularity that no fewer than seven examples survive in preservation.

LEFT: Whilst the WR continued to deliberate about the future new livery for their Western hydraulics, the third, fourth and fifth were outshopped in the standard BR green livery. Later the same year, D1035-D1038 also appeared in this livery. D1035 *Western Yeoman* is approaching Aynho Junction with the 11.40am Birkenhead-Paddington on 29th August 1962. *Photo: M. Mensing*

RIGHT: Carrying the experimental golden ochre livery, D1015 *Western Champion* is preparing to leave Severn Tunnel Junction mpd on 19th May 1964. *Photo: J.N. Simms*

BELOW: Newly painted D1027 *Western Lancer* stands in Swindon Works 'A' shop on 26th January 1964. *Photo: W. Potter*

ABOVE: On 27th April 1967, D9502 passes Lower Soudley with the Cinderford goods. Unusually for a shunting loco, this class carried a four panel route indicator which was required for their operation on main line duties. With wayside goods traffic rapidly disappearing, BR was left with a class of barely used, expensive machinery on its hands. Fortunately, two large industrial concerns, British Steel Corporation and the NCB, found them ideal for their needs and all members of the class were off BR's books only five years after the appearance of D9500. *Photo: W. Potter*

BR Swindon 650hp 0-6-0

Officially designated Type 1 in the main line locomotive category, the D95XXs were primarily designed for shunting and trip working. With the major reduction in sidings and elimination of the pick-up freight under the Beeching Plan, the work for which the class was intended had all but disappeared before the first engine appeared in 1964.

Employed for some time on pick-up freights in the Gloucester and South Wales areas, a batch were reallocated to Hull, but once again there was no work for them to undertake.

With hindsight, it is obvious that the class should never have been built. Withdrawals commenced in April 1968 with 46 of the class subsequently being sold into private industry.

BELOW: Newly constructed D9508 stands outside Swindon Works on 6th September 1964 carrying its attractive livery which included the carriage version of the BR emblem. *Photo: W. Potter*

Later Prototypes

Brush/Maybach 2,800hp Co-Co 'Falcon'

Numbered D0280, the prototype Brush *Falcon* arrived at Finsbury Park depot for service trials on 13th October 1961. Its first duty in revenue earning service came on 16th October when it worked the 6.52am Kings Cross to Cambridge, returning at 10.05am. This trip was repeated later the same day. On October 18th it was used on the 8.15am Kings Cross to Hull which it worked as far as Doncaster. It was on this duty two days later when it suffered a slight fire in a cab heater which resulted in a return to the builders at Loughborough for attention.

The initial livery appeared to be based on the bright shade of green first applied to the skirting of the production version of the English Electric Deltics, with its name enclosed in a falcon silhouette on the bodyside. This colour was offset by panels of light brown on the body work and red buffer beams.

The engines fitted to this locomotive were two Bristol-Siddeley MD655 which were the same as fitted into the Western diesel-hydraulic locomotives, but with a higher degree of supercharging and charge air cooling.

In addition to working in regular service on the GN main line, D0280 underwent various trials throughout the country. On 17th February 1962, it successfully started a twenty coach train from a dead stand on the 1 in 37 Lickey Incline. After transfer for further trials on the WR, D0280 restarted a seventeen coach load on the 1 in 38 of Dainton Bank.

The locomotive was repainted into BR green livery in August 1964 upon completion of its original test period. From November 1964 it was operated by BR without supervision from Brush personnel and was finally sold to BR in January 1971 and repainted in BR blue. Classified as Type 53 and renumbered D1200, much of its final work was secondary duties from Ebbw Junction. Withdrawal came in October 1975.

TOP: The first of three prototype Type 4 designs, the twin-engined Brush *Falcon* is entering Kings Cross with the up Sheffield Pullman in late 1962. *Photo: Colour-Rail*

BOTTOM: Carrying the later BR green livery, *Falcon* is passing Sydney Gardens, Bath with the 1.45pm ex-Paddington on 2nd May 1968. *Photo: Ivo Peters*

English Electric Co 2,700hp Co-Co DP2

The English Electric candidate for higher power second generation Type 4 orders from BR, the 2,700 hp Co-Co, DP2, was introduced on the west coast main line on 14th May 1962, its initial diagram being the 7.45am (SX) Euston to Liverpool, returning with the 2.05pm (SX) Liverpool to Euston.

This locomotive incorporated the charge-cooled version of the English-Electric 16-cylinder CSVT engine, which was originally introduced in the LMS prototypes 10000/10001. Mechanically, DP2 was very similar to English-Electric Deltics, a Co-Co unit well within the specified axle load of eighteen tons and utilising a production Deltic body shell.

After covering over 100,000 miles in traffic without incident, DP2 was generally considered to be the most successful diesel-electric to be operating in Britain. Fifty such machines were considered, especially since the Brush/Sulzer Type 4s were then proving troublesome.

An updated version of DP2 formed the basis for fifty of the D400 class, later Class 50, with flat fronted cabs requested by BR. In retrospect it may have been more appropriate to have constructed 50 locomotives more closely based on the simple form of DP2, but after much modification the 50s have now proved themselves in traffic.

When constructed DP2 did not contain the electronic equipment which later made it so successful. DP2 met its demise on 31st July 1967 when it was involved in a serious accident whilst hauling the 12.00 Kings Cross to Edinburgh just south of Thirsk. Travelling at 80 mph the driver spotted derailed wagons littering the track and although he made an emergency brake application a collision occurred. After a sojourn of one month in York TMD, DP2 was returned to the Vulcan Foundry at Newton-le-Willows where it was deemed to be beyond economic repair and broken up the following year.

LEFT: Prior to the application of the full Deltic livery, DP2 is receiving attention at Camden shed in July 1962. It is carrying the earlier plain green livery with yellow ends. *Photo: G. Rixon*

Birmingham Railway Carriage & Wagon Co 2,750hp Co-Co 'Lion'

Built as a private venture by a consortium which included Associated Electrical Industries, the Birmingham Railway Carriage & Wagon Company and Sulzer Brothers (London) Ltd, the locomotive *Lion* was the first medium-speed-engine prototype to conform to BRs requirements for a second generation Type 4 six-axle diesel locomotive of at least 2,500 hp.

With the abolition of the British Transport Commission in the reorganisation of the 1962 Transport Act, the BR design panel requested industrial designers Wilkes and Ashmore to prepare a specification for the new look for future locomotives. *Lion* closely followed the design panel's recommendations except that it was finished in a striking overall white livery.

After initial trials between Wolverhampton and Shrewsbury, D0260 entered regular traffic on 14th May 1962 when it worked the following diagram. Commencing with the 7.25am Wolverhampton to Paddington it returned as far as Wolverhampton with the 12.10pm Paddington to Birkenhead, then took a second trip to London on the 3.35pm Wolverhampton to Paddington, returning to Wolverhampton with the 7.10pm Paddington to Shrewsbury.

Unfortunately, *Lion* did not come up to BR's needs and BRCW, which was in the throes of financial collapse, declined BR's offer to assist in the production of the 500+ new standard Type 4s. It was then that BR approached Brush to produce an alternative to *Lion* which would be nearer to their requirements. This decision eventually resulted in the construction of the 512 Brush/Sulzer 2,750 hp locomotives.

Brush/Sulzer 3946hp Co-Co 'Kestrel'

By the mid-1960s, the Deltics were showing their prowess on the east coast main line and the pro-Deltic lobby was producing designs for a 4,400 hp version. Whilst these eventually came to nothing, Sulzer was also showing interest in producing a more powerful high speed diesel locomotive. Eventually, in collaboration with Brush, it produced the 4,000 hp prototype *Kestrel* as a private venture. This impressive machine left the Brush works at Loughborough on 20th January 1968, travelling to Derby Works for weighing and inspection.

Design consultants Wilkes and Ashmore had once again advised on the outward appearance, giving the cabs a more streamlined form with a view towards high speed operation. The livery chosen for *Kestrel* was a striking combination of grey roof, golden yellow body above the waistline and chocolate brown below.

Trial workings were based on Shirebrook where it worked a series of diagrams from Mansfield Colliery sidings to Whitemoor. Subsequent trials during September 1968 involved a circular Derby-Stoke-Crewe-Nuneaton-Leicester-Derby working when the load consisted of Dynamometer Car M45049 and Mobile Test Unit No 3 M45055.

This potential Type 5 locomotive was never taken up by BR whose traction policies were leading them towards both the introduction of diesel-multiple units for High Speed Train operation and the need for a different breed of locomotive for future heavy duty freight traffic. With the lack of interest from BR this prototype was exported to the USSR in 1975.

ABOVE: In spotless white livery, D0260 *Lion* is passing Tyseley with the 12.10pm Paddington-Birmingham in June 1962. Whilst *Lion* matched exactly the specifications laid down by the BRB, it remains a mystery why BRCW went into liquidation instead of undertaking to build for BR.
Photo: Colour-Rail/M. Mensing

ABOVE: Looking somewhat well used, HS4000 *Kestrel* is at Hull Dairycoates depot whilst undergoing trials on the ER. Privately sponsored by Hawker Siddeley, this design was not taken up by BR. *Photo: N.E. Preedy*

Standard Designs

Birmingham Railway Carriage & Wagon Co 1,550hp Bo-Bo Type 3

The first of an order for 98 locomotives of this class from Birmingham Railway Carriage & Wagon Company arrived at Hither Green on 17th December 1959. Primarily designed for use on freight traffic, the type basically followed that of the BRCW D5300 class, but due to the elimination of the steam train heating boiler and its anciliary equipment, it was possible to install an eight cylinder Sulzer engine with no overall increase in locomotive weight, this being the first class of locomotives to be fitted with eth from new.

After introduction of the BRCW Type 3s, the LM Type 2s were retained on the SR for a period to provide train heating as the SR did not then have any electrically heated stock. Most trains were formed with the Type 2 coupled inside the BRCW loco. Instead of using a steam train heating boiler, the locomotives were fitted with electrical train heating; the few winter diagrams intended for these engines meant that only a small number of coaches needed conversion to electrical heating. On 3rd December 1963, two BRCW diesels arrived at Bromford Bridge on a train of 54 tank wagons from Fawley, this being the forerunner of five trains each week, replacing the previous trains of twenty five wagons.

The first member of the class to be fitted for push-pull working, D6580, was tested on 21st July 1965 when it worked two trips between Basingstoke and Wimbledon Park. These tests were successful and regular services were introduced with TC sets in July 1967. Becoming BR Class 33 under the TOPS system, 69 survive in traffic at May 1988.

TOP: Passing Norton Halt, BRCW Type 3 D6508 is about to take the Evesham to Oxford line at Norton Junction with an up Esso tank train on 24th August 1963. *Photo: M. Mensing*

BOTTOM: Before the addition of yellow warning panels, D6506 is at Basingstoke mpd alongside the preserved Standard Class 4 75078. A 9th September 1962 picture. *Photo: W. Potter*

English Electric Co 1,750hp Co-Co Type 3

Closely resembling in outline the English-Electric Type 4s, the first of an initial batch of 30 locomotives, D6700, entered service on the Great Eastern line shortly before Christmas 1960. It was fitted with a single four-stroke engine diesel engine rated at 1,750 hp, a twelve-cylinder version of the V16 2,000 hp engine used in the Type 4s. Turbo-charged by two Napier exhaust gas driven turbo chargers, the Type 3 incorporates an intercooler which reduces the temperature of the charge air before it enters the cylinders.

By the end of February 1961, the early members of the class had been employed on dynamometer car trials on the Cambridge main line, the trains being formed of 25 to 38 'Minfits'. Included in the make up of the train was a vehicle identified as a 'diesel brake tender' which had been borrowed from the Scottish Region. This vehicle had been constructed from a short wheelbase carriage underframe to provide additional braking power on diesel hauled unfitted trains.

Maids of all work, the EE Type 3s were well received by the operating departments and eventually numbered a total of 309 locomotives incorporating two different body designs. Now designated BR class 37, they are equally at home on express passenger work or heavy freight duties and remain at the forefront of the BR diesel power fleet.

ABOVE: The introduction of the EE Type 3s on the WR heralded the beginning of the end for diesel-hydraulic traction. D6853 is passing Fishguard with a mixed freight on 15th August 1963. *Photo: D.A. Codling*

BELOW: Some two years later and also on the WR, D6990 is between duties outside Radyr mpd on 31st July 1965. *Photo: W. Potter*

English Electric Co 'Deltic' 3,300hp Co-Co Type 5

In April 1958, following the success of the prototype Deltic, an order was placed for a further twenty-two locomotives in the class. Classified as Type 5, these engines were originally planned as D1000 to D1021, although in the event they were allocated numbers D9000 to D9021. The first to arrive at Doncaster for acceptance trials was D9001 on 17th January 1961, a corner of the works being set aside as a stabling point during their trials, pending allocation to permanent quarters on the east coast route. On its second trial trip, D9001 touched 100 mph down Stoke Bank with a load of fourteen bogies.

The second locomotive in this series to arrive at Doncaster was D9000 on 28th February which had the misfortune of being rammed by a pilot engine within sight of the works, although it was back on trial within a few days. D9000 was temporarily equipped with a fixed beam light as an experiment intended to give some warning of approach to permanent way men.

A system of double section block working was introduced for trials in the up direction, with the same bell signal, four-pause-four, which was used for the Silver Jubilee and Coronation workings before the Second World War. At the same time, existing distant signals were converted from semaphore to colour light, and set back pending the introduction of the new timetable when all of the Deltics were to enter traffic.

The early production Deltics had been built with fabricated bogie frames similar to those on the D67XX series and subject to cracking, a problem which delayed the production schedule of the remaining members of the class while they were fitted with bogies manufactured incorporating cast steel frames. The final locomotive in the series, D9021, arrived at Doncaster for acceptance trials on 21st March 1962, being directly allocated to Haymarket, where its first passenger duty was the up Heart of Midlothian on 3rd May.

For over twenty years, the Deltics achieved a very high utilisation on the east coast route, being at the forefront of diesel electric traction. Like the A3s and A4s before them, the Deltics attracted a cult following with no fewer than six examples being preserved, in addition to the prototype.

OPPOSITE: Yet to be named and carrying the two tone green livery, D9005 heads a Newcastle-Kings Cross express south of Grantham in April 1962. *Photo: K.R. Pirt/K.R. Photographics*

ABOVE: Before the introduction of yellow warning panels, D9007 *Pinza* is working the down Heart of Midlothian near Marshalls Meadow, Berwick on Tweed. A 23rd May 1962 picture. *Photo: M. Mensing*

LEFT: After the class received names, it was necessary to move the BR emblem from the centre of the bodyside to the cab, two smaller versions being used, one each end below the numbers. The nameplate of D9004 *Queen's Own Highlander* was photographed at Haymarket on 30th May 1966. *Photo: M.S. Welch*

Clayton Equipment Co 900hp Bo-Bo Type 1

With three different classes of Type 1 main-line diesel-electric locomotives already in service (D80XX, D82XX & D84XX), BR decided that future requirements in this power range be built to a new Bo-Bo design. An order for eighty-eight locomotives was placed with the Clayton Equipment Co. of Hatton, Derby, the design incorporating two 450 hp Davey-Paxman engines placed each side of a full width central driving cab.

Delivery of the prototype 900 hp D8500 took place at Marylebone on 26th July 1962, the locomotive returning to Derby the next day. Intended for use on the Scottish Region, D8500 arrived at Polmadie on 10th September 1962, replacing the veteran Jumbos on their various trip workings.

On 5th September 1963, D8500/1 worked in tandem on a trial iron-ore train from Tyne Dock to Consett, further trials being conducted later in the month on coal trains over the Blyth and Tyne section. On 4th December that year, newly delivered D8555 was a runaway casualty whilst working trip E58 of 36 wagons on the Loanhead branch, becoming derailed and causing a line blockage.

The 'Claytons', as they became known, were never a success. Major problems with the Paxman engines resulted in availability being as low as 50% and their problems reached such a pitch that newly built locomotives were being placed directly into store. Coupled with this problem, the work for which they were designed, namely light to medium freight, was disappearing as a result of the Beeching Plan.

When BRB's National Traction Plan was implemented, the Claytons were early victims and all were withdrawn by the end of 1971, only one example, D8568, remaining in preservation.

LEFT: Clayton Type 1 D8613 is portrayed with Midland 4F 43953 at Glapwell Colliery on 16th October 1965. As the last Midland-designed tender engine, 43953 was taking part in the Midland Locomotive Requiem Rail Tour. D8613 had been attached to the rear of the train at Seymour Junction while 43953 ran round to act as pilot over the adverse grades to the colliery sidings. *Photo: J.N. Simms*

BELOW: Centre cab Claytons D8509 and D8522 leave Cark & Cartmel with a four coach extra on 21st June 1968. *Photo: M. Mensing*

Brush/Sulzer 2,750hp (now 2,580hp), 2,650hp Co-Co Type 4

With every generation of railway locomotives, there is always one design, which because of its ability to perform well across a whole range of duties, is subsequently constructed in large numbers. In the diesel-electric generation this title must go to the Brush/Sulzer Type 4, which in all of its variations totalled 512 locomotives.

The first member of this class, D1500, made its debut on 6th September 1962 when it travelled from the Brush locomotive works at Loughborough to Crewe for weighing. On 2nd November 1962, D1500 was transferred to Swindon where it was used on trials with a dynamometer car, its first duty in traffic being the 6.55am from Cheltenham to Paddington which it took over at Swindon, returning at 1.30pm with the Plymouth parcels. Subsequent tests were successfully carried out on 20th February 1963 when D1500 moved a sixteen coach load from a dead stand on Dainton Bank.

Initially, the first batch of Brush Type 4s proved to be no more reliable than any other diesel classes and from 25th October 1963, D1546 and D1547 were worked continuously on six Finsbury Park diagrams until they failed, the object being to attempt to estimate and then eliminate the teething problems which had plagued the early batch.

By January 1965, several of the class were transferred from the GN to the GE where they replaced the English Electric Type 4s taking over the Liverpool Street to Norwich workings.

During their service on BR there have been numerous detail differences in this class as they have been modified for a variety of reasons. Having given sterling service for many years, most are still in traffic due to the refurbishment programme being carried out by Crewe works.

LEFT: Two tone green Brush Type 4 D1547 passes Farm Grounds after leaving Sheffield Midland with an up express in July 1966. *Photo: K.R. Pirt/K.R. Photographics*

ABOVE: After returning from tests on the WR, D1500 is inside Finsbury Park depot in March 1963. *Photo: Roy Hobbs*

RIGHT: Still in grey primer, D1580 undergoes electrical testing at Crewe Works on 26th April 1964. *Photo: T.B. Owen*

ABOVE: 1964 saw the introduction of the experimental XP64 train set which incorporated many new ideas for passenger comfort. For publicity purposes Brush/Sulzer Type 4 D1733 was painted in a turquoise livery to match the XP64 stock. Initially it carried a red cabside panel with the new BR logo which was removed after publicity pictures had been taken. D1733 is at Cardiff General station on 31st July 1965. *Photo: W. Potter*

English Electric Co 'Warship' 2,700hp Co-Co Type 4

By March 1964, Crewe Works had ceased to give general overhauls to steam locomotives, the largest being a heavy intermediate. Concurrently, most locomotive depots were running down their steam locomotives and the condition of many deteriorated due to inferior maintenance. Depots such as Carlisle Kingmoor often had as many as thirty engines stopped for repairs. As a stop gap, before full electrification on the LM west coast main line between Weaver Junction and Glasgow, fifty English Electric locomotives were ordered. These 2,700 hp machines, based on the design of the privately sponsored prototype, DP2, were the final example of high speed mixed traffic diesel electric locomotives to be built for BR.

By 1st October 1967, the first locomotive in this class, D400, had arrived at Crewe from the Vulcan Foundry at Newton-le-Willows for acceptance trials. In addition to the usual works plates, D400 carried a small oval plate inscribed 'This locomotive is the property of English Electric Holdings Limited', who leased them to BR.

During February 1968, D402 had arrived at Polmadie for crew training. The multiple control jumpers were not fitted on locomotives D402-D449 although wiring was installed for subsequent fitting. Having been introduced into regular traffic, sister engine D401 was working the down Royal Scot on 25th April 1968 when it came to grief only a mile short of its goal when it was derailed at a pair of facing points at the north end of Eglinton Street station. With local services more or less at a standstill, the Polmadie and Eastfield cranes had D401 rerailed by 21.00.

Once electrification was energised between Weaver Junction and Glasgow, the class was transferred to Western Region, a move which began in late 1972. The locomotives were in relatively poor shape due to 100 mph thrashings they had received on the LM. After some high speed running between Bristol and London, a number of weaknesses were found and a major program of refurbishment was carried out by Doncaster works.

Eventually receiving names of warships, the class was designated Type 50 and at the time of writing continues to give good service on WR services and on the Waterloo to Exeter route.

ABOVE: Carrying the rail blue livery with yellow ends from new, D416 passes Shap Wells with 1S76 on 15th August 1970. *Photo: Peter Fitton*

BELOW: D414 joins the west coast main line with 1A14 at Morecambe South Junction on 17th July 1968. *Photo: Peter Fitton*

Shunters

Numerous types were introduced. Here are three examples.

British Railways 204hp 0-6-0 Diesel Mechanical

Standard version of the diesel-mechanical design, D2082 is portrayed working the Weymouth tramway on 22nd July 1966; and it is sporting the obligatory yellow and black ends to its green livery. After ordering a variety of examples from private suppliers, BR introduced its standard design which was later designated class 03 under the TOPS system. Because of its proven service, the Gardner engine was chosen and in many respects the class resembled the design produced by the Drewry Car Co. Prior to construction of the first example at Swindon, it had been planned to fit a steam locomotive type chimney complete with copper cap. This was frowned upon by the BTC who issued a directive to remove it from the drawing. *Photo: C.G. Maggs*

Hudswell Clarke 204hp 0-6-0 Diesel Mechanical

As they were introduced five years after the standard BR version, one can only speculate what reasons lay behind the construction of the ten members of this class. Although the body style had a smart appearance, they never received the TOPS numbers and all were withdrawn in 1967. After a period of use with the NCB, two examples survive in preservation on the Keighley and Worth Valley Railway. Shortly before withdrawal, D2513 is pictured outside Derby motive power depot on 23rd March 1967. *Photo: K. Fairey*

Ruston & Hornsby 275hp 0-6-0 Diesel Electric

Resplendent in its stylish SR malachite green livery, D2996 marshals a heater van outside Southampton Dock motive power depot on 19th June 1965. Ordered specifically for use in the SR's Southampton Dock complex, these neat looking diesel-electric locomotives replaced the USA 0-6-0T shunting engines which had worked the docks since 1946. Being somewhat heavier than the 0-6-0 diesel mechanicals, they represented a compromise between the large 0-6-0 diesel-mechanical classes 08/9 and the smaller class 03/4s.

With the introduction of container traffic which replaced wagon load operation, the Southampton Docks railway system was run down, these engines, later designated 07, being made redundant by 1977. *Photo: W. Potter*

LEFT: The distinctive crest of the prototype twin-engined Brush *Falcon*. This is its second livery, standard BR green/pale grey with yellow warning panels, applied between the initial lime green/brown scheme and its final BR corporate blue. *Photo: Geoff Rixon*

BELOW: Photographed at Woking on 31st July 1965, the nameplate of D803 *Albion* shows the traditional serif style of lettering much favoured by Swindon, dating back to the days of Brunel and the GWR. *Photo: J.D. Gomersall*